LET'S LEARN ABOUT MATH

LET'S MEASURE

BY CRYSTAL SIKKENS

TABLE OF CONTENTS

A Crabtree Seedlings Book

Crabtree Publishing

crabtreebooks.com

School-to-Home Support for Caregivers and Teachers

This book helps children grow by letting them practice reading. Here are a few guiding questions to help the reader build comprehension skills. Possible answers appear here in red.

Before Reading:

- What do I know about measurement?
    - *I know measurement is about finding out how much something weighs.*
    - *I know measurement is about finding out how tall something is.*
- What do I want to learn about measurement?
    - *I want to learn the difference between measuring height and length.*
    - *I want to learn what capacity is.*

During Reading:

- What have I learned so far?
    - *I have learned that measuring height is finding out how tall something is.*
    - *I have learned that length is measuring how long something is.*
- I wonder why...
    - *I wonder why measurement helps us describe an object.*
    - *I wonder why you can use a smaller object to measure a larger one.*

After Reading:

- What did I learn about measurement?
    - *I have learned that measurements help us compare objects.*
    - *I have learned that capacity is how much something can hold.*
- Read the book again and look for the glossary words.
    - *I see the word* ***measurement*** *on page 3 and the word* ***length*** *on page 4. The other vocabulary words are found on pages 22 and 23.*

We use **measurement** everyday. Measurement can help us describe objects.

We can find out how long something is by measuring its **length**.

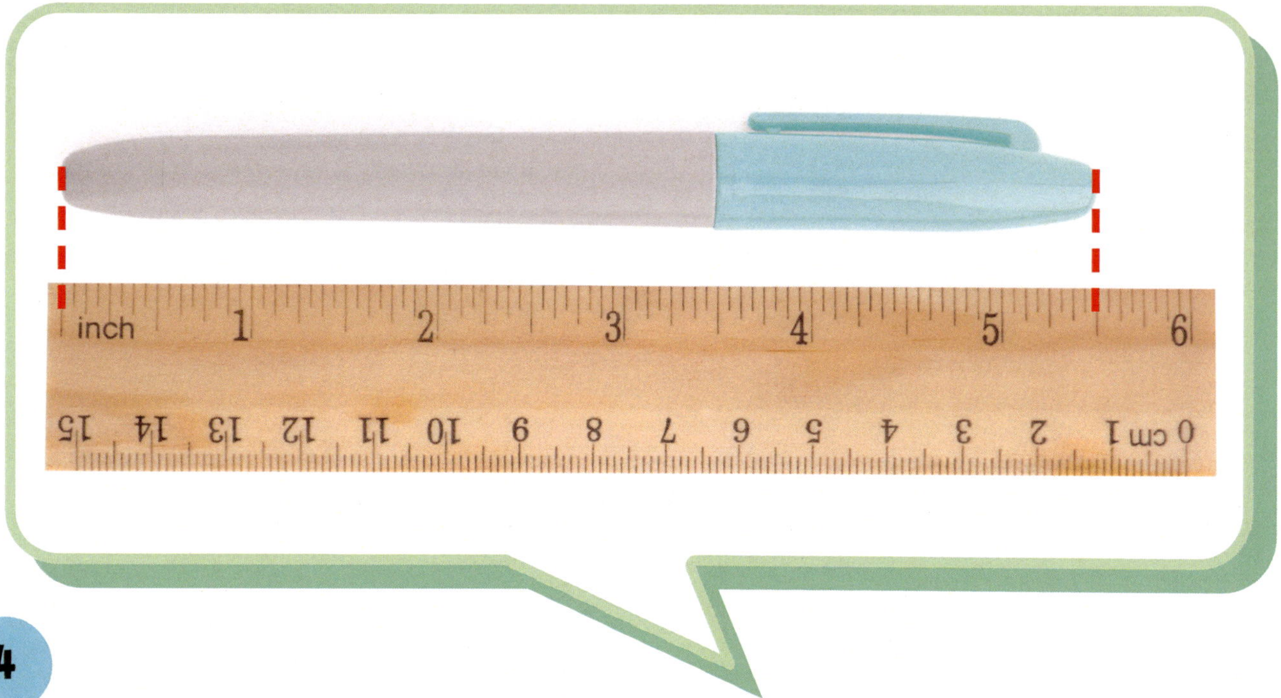

When we measure how tall something is, we measure its **height**.

We measure **weight** to find out how heavy something is.

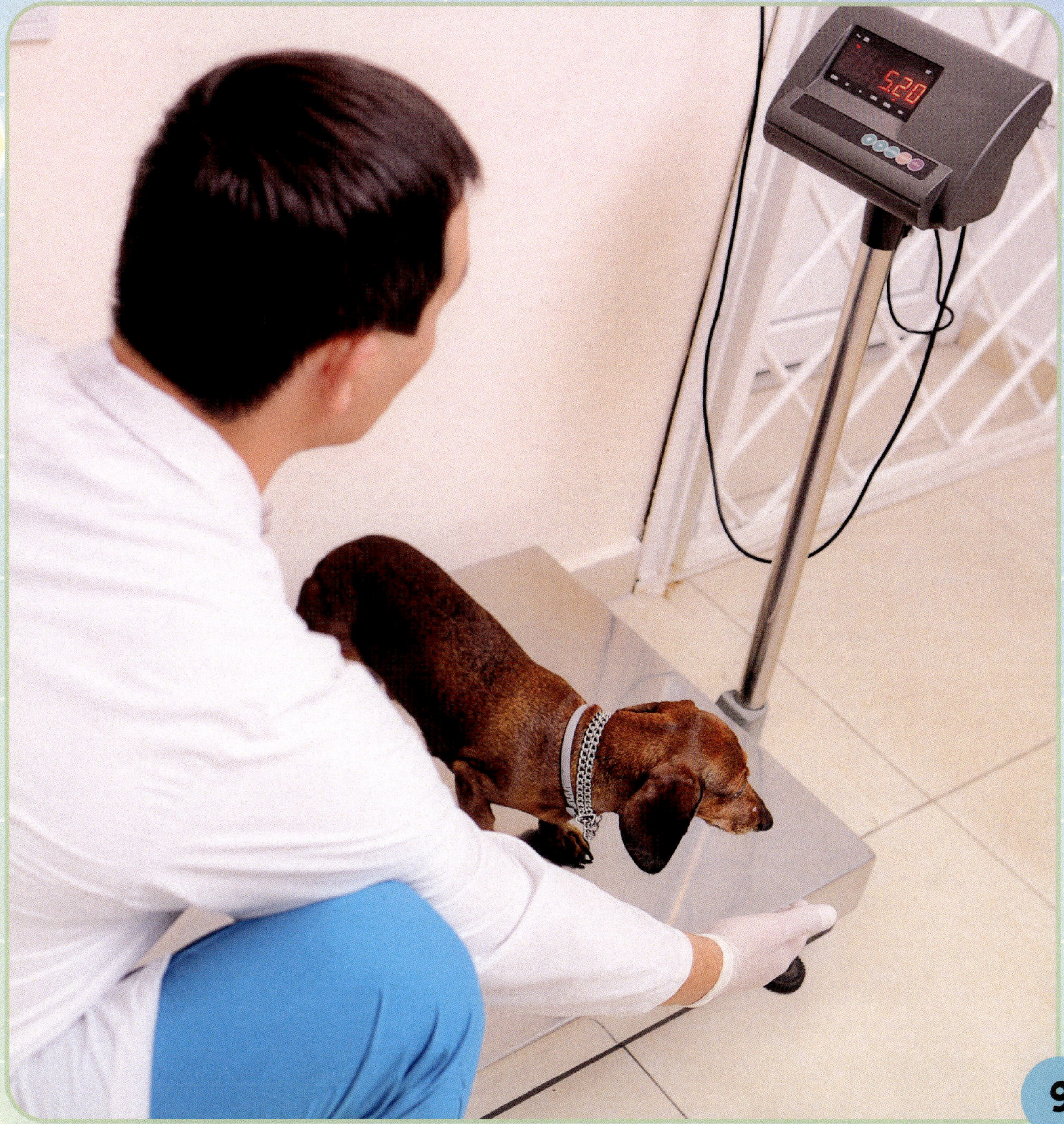
5.20

When we want to find out how much something can hold, we measure its **capacity**.

Measuring can help us **compare** objects.

A watermelon is heavier than an apple. A watermelon weighs more.

We can measure length
to compare objects.

The pencil is the longest.
The paperclip is the shortest.

Can you put these vegetables in order from longest to shortest?

We can have fun by measuring the length of one object with a smaller object.

This eggplant is 5 baby carrots long.

Use baby carrots to find the lengths of these foods. Which one is the longest?

GLOSSARY

capacity (kuh-PASS-i-tee): The amount that a container can hold

compare (kuhm-PAIR): To examine two or more items to find something similar

height (hahyt): The distance from bottom to top

length (lengkth): The distance from one side to the other

measurement (MEZH-er-muhnt): The process of finding out the size, weight, or amount of something by measuring

weight (weyt): A measure of how heavy something is

INDEX

ABOUT THE AUTHOR

Crystal Sikkens has been helping create books for Crabtree Publishing for over 20 years. In her spare time, she loves spending time with her husband and children on their family farm.

Written by: Crystal Sikkens
Editor: Kathy Middleton
Designed by: Samara Parent
Photographs: All images from Shutterstock
Production manager: Candice Campbell

Crabtree Publishing

crabtreebooks.com 800-387-7650

Hardcover: 978-1-0398-7275-2
Paperback: 978-1-0398-7333-9
Ebook (pdf): 978-1-0398-7389-6
Epub: 978-1-0398-7438-1

Published in Canada
Crabtree Publishing
616 Welland Avenue
St. Catharines, Ontario
L2M 5V6

Published in the United States
Crabtree Publishing
347 Fifth Avenue
Suite 1402-145
New York, New York, 10016

Library and Archives Canada Cataloguing in Publication
Available at Library and Archives Canada

Library of Congress Cataloging-in-Publication Data
Available at the Library of Congress

Printed in the U.S.A./CP032026